Speak Latin

First Steps Toward Conversation in the Classroom

Speak Latin

First Steps Toward Conversation in the Classroom

Felipe Vogel
T. Michael W. Halcomb

GlossaHouse
Wilmore, KY
GlossaHouse.com

Speak Latin: First Steps Toward Conversation in the Classroom

GlossaHouse, LLC
110 Callis Circle
Wilmore, KY 40390

Vogel, Felipe.
 Speak Latin : first steps toward conversation in the classroom /
 Felipe Vogel, T. Michael W. Halcomb. – Wilmore, KY :
 GlossaHouse, ©2017.

        xvii, 29 pages ; 20 cm.
        (LAETA)

        Includes bibliographical references (pages 28-29).
        ISBN 978-1942697398 (paperback)

        1. Latin language -- Conversation and phrase books --
        English. 2. Latin language -- Pronunciation.   I. Title. II.
        Series. III. Halcomb, T. Michael W.

        PA2017.V63 2017   478.3/421   2017XXXXXX

The fonts used to create this work are available from
www.linguistsoftware.com/lgku.htm

Cover Design by T. Michael W. Halcomb
Book Layout & Design by T. Michael W. Halcomb & Felipe Vogel

To our teachers and colleagues at the University of Kentucky

LAETA

Latin: Ancient Educational Tools & Aids

SERIES EDITOR
T. Michael W. Halcomb

LAETA

The Latin term *LAETA* is an adjective that means "fertile" or "welcoming," especially when describing land. It is also a term that captures the link between this series and its Hebrew (HA'ARETS) and Greek (AGROS) counterparts also bearing land-related names and published by GlossaHouse. In keeping with those series, *LAETA* functions as an acronym: Latin: Ancient Educational Tools & Aids. This series exists because, while there are many great resources on Latin, more can and always will need to be created. Thus, *LAETA* welcomes new and innovative works, those that make a contribution, however big or small, to the journey of learning Latin. The long-term aim is to create a tiered curriculum suite featuring innovative readers, grammars, specialized studies, and similar resources that will both encourage and foster the use of Latin. Additionally, the *LAETA* series endeavors to facilitate the creation and publication of innovative and inexpensive print and digital resources within the context of the global community.

TABLE OF CONTENTS

Introduction

Finis ab origine pendet. This ancient Roman proverb excerpted in part from Manilius can be translated "The end depends on the beginning." This is quite apropos to this book. This is the case because our vision for *Speak Latin* is to see it used as a beginner's resource, one that will help teachers and students take the first step in incorporating spoken Latin in the classroom. Of course, this work can be used by individuals studying on their own, but we are confident that it will likely bear the most fruit when put to use in a group setting.

It is important to note here at the outset that this book is not an attempt to reinvent the wheel. It is not, for example, an attempt to replace grammars, lexicons, and other helpful study aids. If anything, it is meant to supplement such works. In some sense, then, this work is not all that innovative. Rather, it stands in the long line and tradition of Latin works that precede it. What may be novel, however, is simply the pared down selection and arrangement of the content.

Even then, the arrangement is a somewhat modified version of the Koine Greek counterpart to this work: *Speak Koine Greek* (GlossaHouse, 2014). Thus, the main body of the book follows a tripartite structure based on how discourse works: "Starting the Conversation," "Continuing the Conversation," and "Ending the Conversation." We hope this layout results in a user-friendly experience with the book.

To this we have added a few more sections that basically form bookends. The first addition, consisting mainly of prefatory material, contains the alphabet and offers different pronunciation options. The second addition is found in the appendix and there we discuss several teaching tips for the classroom, such as choosing a Latin name and strategies for asking and answering questions. We also provide a bibliography consisting of both works consulted and works recommended, some digital and some print.

As stated above, our main hope is to see this employed in the Latin classroom as a beginner's resource. For that reason, we have purposefully kept this size of the book small. This makes it more inviting, less intimidating, and easier to navigate. An added bonus is that this also allows the book to be very affordable.

For teachers wishing to use this book, one approach would be for a teacher to look through the entire book and simply choose words and phrases that will best fit their lesson plans or work best in the flow of their curriculum and then implement them. Since this book does not follow say, *Wheelock's Latin* or any other grammar, we anticipate that educators will likely have to adopt a pick-and-choose method. To that end, we are certainly open to hearing what might or might not have worked in your particular context.

There are a few choices we have made in creating this book that should be noted. First, words and phrases are not in alphabetical order by English (except in the "Classroom Items" section), because we wanted to give prominence to the Latin, which we have placed first in each entry. Moreover, may words and phrases are often grouped into small bits of discourse and, as a result, there was no way of alphabetizing them. Yet, to make English words easier to find, we bolded and italicized them throughout.

We also included genitive endings, along with the grammatical genders of words, beside individual vocabulary terms. As a result, words in phrases or sentences and, of course, indeclinables, will not have this data. Another choice we made was to indicate syllable stress with accent marks. We chose not to use macrons because, from our perspective, including macrons along with stress marks could be somewhat redundant with regard to indicating syllable stress.

On the one hand, including macrons would clarify vowel length or quantity but, on the other hand, insisting that vowel quantity be pronounced may be discouraging to beginners. Thus, here we attempt to emphasize, first and foremost, learning proper stress and stress patterns. In the future, we hope to create audio files to accompany this resource. We hope that will further aid learners in their endeavors.

Finally, because there have always been at least a few Latin speakers from Roman times until the present, terms not attested in ancient texts have always been used. For instance, the Latin word "computer," which we list as either *machina computatoria* or *computatrum*, is a recent neologism. We have included only a few such terms and, where we have, have made sure to consult multiple reliable sources (see the bibliography).

We realize that the decisions stated above may draw criticism but our hope is that, at the end of the day, these choices make the book easier to use. To reiterate, our hope is that teachers and students will find this beginner's resource helpful. While seasoned educators may discover that it works well for their classrooms, in no sense do we view this resource as a go-to research aid for them. The audience squarely in focus, borne in mind during every decision made, consists of new learners and those teaching them. And so, if that is you, we wish you the best as you embark on this fun and amazing journey. And since we started with a Roman proverb, let's end with one: *Carpe diem!* (Seize the day!)

Pentecost, 2017
Felipe Vogel
T. Michael W. Halcomb

The Latin Alphabet & Pronunciation(s)

Letters	Restored Classical	Ecclesiastical
Aa	f<u>a</u>ther	
Bb	<u>b</u>oy	
Cc	<u>c</u>at	c or cc before e, ae, oe, i, y: <u>ch</u>urch sc before e, ae, oe, i, y: <u>sh</u>ed
Dd	<u>d</u>og	
Ee	<u>e</u>lephant	
Ff	<u>f</u>ig	
Gg	<u>g</u>irl	before e, ae, i, y: gara<u>g</u>e gn: se<u>ni</u>or, French "si<u>gn</u>or"
Hh	<u>h</u>im	aspirated "k" sound in *mihi* and *nihil* and their compounds, similar to German "a<u>ch</u>t"; otherwise mute
Ii	ma<u>chi</u>ne (if short, often p<u>i</u>t)	(written as Jj)
Ii (initial Y intervocalic)	<u>y</u>o<u>y</u>o	
Kk	<u>c</u>at	
Ll	<u>l</u>ove	
Mm	<u>m</u>om	
Nn	<u>n</u>o	
Oo	<u>o</u>rder (if long, often dr<u>o</u>ne)	
Pp	<u>p</u>uppy	
Qq	<u>q</u>ueen	
Rr	trilled, as in Spanish "¡A<u>rr</u>iba!"	

Ss	<u>s</u>ound	between vowels: <u>z</u>ebra
Tt	<u>t</u>ail	ti = /tsi/ as in Pat<u>sy</u> before a vowel and preceded by any letter except s, t or x
Vv	<u>w</u>ay	<u>v</u>ery
Xx	ta<u>x</u>i	
Yy	front close vowel y (French "au j<u>u</u>s")	mach<u>i</u>ne
Zz	<u>z</u>oo	be<u>ds</u>

Vowel pairs		
ae	<u>ai</u>sle	<u>e</u>lephant
au	h<u>ou</u>se	
ei	<u>ei</u>ght only in *hei*, otherwise two syllables: pa<u>yee</u> in *mei*	
eu	e + u pronounced rapidly as a single syllable, as in Spanish "<u>Eu</u>ropa", /ew.ˈrɔ.pɐ/	
oe	c<u>oy</u>	<u>e</u>lephant

Consonant Clusters		
ch	either German "a<u>ch</u>t" or blo<u>ckh</u>ead	<u>c</u>at
ph	either <u>f</u>oot or u<u>ph</u>ill	<u>f</u>oot
th	either <u>th</u>eater or ho<u>th</u>ouse	<u>t</u>oe

The Latin alphabet consists of 23 letters. These letters are listed on the preceding pages in the standard order in which they appear. Because there are two leading and, perhaps, competing pronunciations used by Latin teachers across the world, we have opted to provide both. Apart from the fact that providing both pronunciation frameworks, namely, the Restored and Ecclesiastical, allows one to see the similarities and differences between the two, it likewise mitigates against alienating someone based on their preference. We should say, too, that while we have only provided two possibilities, more exist. Indeed, in many contexts across the globe, the native phonological inventories of any variety of speakers often colors the way they might pronounce Latin.

In the preceding table the "Restored Classical" pronunciation is what can be found in many grammars and textbooks concerned with the Classical Era. Likewise, the "Ecclesiastical," which is post-Classical and therefore much later, is offered. For both, we provide the letters and their associated sounds in each system, while also giving English examples with approximate sounds. Sometimes, however, the sounds of either Latin system do not really exist in English; thus, we had to draw from other languages, such as French, German, Spanish, and even the International Phonetic Alphabet (IPA).

If the approximations and descriptions here don't quite get you to where you need with regard to pronunciation, please consult another grammar, such as that written by Henle or, perhaps, Wheelock, for Classical. See Collins for Ecclesiastical. Likewise, as noted above, we hope to have accompanying audio files for this work in the near future. If and when that possibility becomes a reality, we would commend using that resource as well. Please note that in the preceding pronunciation guide, the underlined letters in each of the words are the sounds we associate with the letters in the left-most "Letters" column.

Before Starting: Some Go-To Phrases

Non intéllego.
I don't understand.

Dic íterum, quaeso.
Say that again, please.

Quid dixísti?
What did you say?

Loquerísne Latíne?
Do you speak Latin?

Quómodo ___ Latíne dícitur?
How do you say ___ in Latin?

Néscio.
I don't know.

Quid ___ sibi vult?
What does ___ mean?

Loquerísne Ánglice?
Do you speak English?

Ánglice, quaeso.
In English, please.

Licétne mihi exíre / locum secrétum pétere?
May I leave / go to the restroom?

Ignósce mihi. / Ignóscite mihi.
Forgive me. (I'm sorry.)

Grátias tibi ago.
Thank you.
Libénter.
You're welcome. / My pleasure.

Benígne.
No, thanks.

Sic / Ita.
Yes.

Mínime.
No.

When answering questions, a restatement in the negative is common:
Gaudésne?
Are you happy?
Non gaúdeo.
I'm not happy.

Dóleo.
I'm sorry. (lit. "I'm sad.")

Pro dolor! / Eheu!
Oh, no! / Alas! / Unfortunately, ...
Senésco. Pro dolor!
Unfortunately I'm getting old.

Starting the Conversation

A. Greetings

Salve, discípule (aut discípula)!
Hello, student! (-e/-a: vocative singular masculine/feminine distinguishes between male and female students)

Salvéte, discípuli et discípulae (linguae Latinae)
Hello, students (of the Latin language)!

Salve, magíster (aut magístra)!
Hello, teacher! (again, masculine or feminine)

Bonum diem!
Good morning!

Heus!
Hey!

Quid est tibi nomen?
What's your name?
Nomen mihi est Marcus / Iúlia.
My name is Mark / Julie.

Quid agis?
How are you?
Óptime! / Bene! / Satis bene.
Great! / Good! / So-so or Okay.
Péssime! / Non bene! / Male!
Terrible! / Not good! / Bad!
Et tu?
And you?

Quómodo te habes? / Quómodo vos habétis?
How are you doing? / How are you all doing?

B. Getting to Know Someone: Initial Questions and Requests

Unde ortus es? / Ubi natus es? / Cuias es?
Where are you from?
Novi Eboráci ortus sum. / Novi Eboráci natus sum.
I am from New York. / I was born in New York.

Ubi hábitas?
Where do you live?
Novi Eboráci hábito. *(locative case looks like the genitive in 1st &
2nd declension singular)*
I live in New York.
Carthágine hábito. *(locative case looks like the ablative in 3rd
declension singular & plural)*
I live in Carthage.
Athénis hábito. *(locative case looks like the ablative/dative in 2nd
declension plural)*
I live in Athens.

Quo múnere fúngeris?
What is your job? (lit. "What job do you perform?")
Magíster sum.
I am a teacher.

Quot annos natus es?
How old are you?
Decem annos natus sum.
I am ten years old.

Placéntne tibi lardum? *(-ne is affixed to the first word of a question)*
Do you like bacon?

Placet mihi lardum.
I like bacon.

Placéntne tibi lardum et ova?
Do you like bacon and eggs?
Placet mihi lardum et ova.
I like bacon and eggs.

Placétne tibi lardum an caro gallinácea?
Do you like bacon or chicken?
Dísplicet mihi caro gallinácea.
I do not like chicken.

Continuing the Conversation:

A. Classroom-related Terms (right column ordered by English)

Sárcina, ae, f.	*Bag (backpack)*
Liber, libri, m.	*Book*
Sella, ae, f.	*Chair*
Caput, cápita, n.	*Chapter*
Schola, ae, f.	*Class, lesson*
Cursus scholárum	*Class, course*
Concláve scholásticum	*Classroom*
Máchina computatória / computatórium	*Computer*
Mensa, ae, f.	*Desk*
Perículum, i, n. / Probátio, probatiónis, f.	*Exam, test*
Probatiónem subíre	*To take a test*
Exémplum, i, n.	*Example*
Pensum, i, n.	*Homework*
Página, ae, f.	*Page*
Charta, ae, f.	*Paper*
Cálamus, i, m.	*Pen*
Gráphium, i, n.	*Pencil*
Imágo, imáginis, f.	*Picture*
Telephónum, i, n.	*Phone*
Locus secrétus	*Restroom*
Ludus, i, m.	*School (lower)*
Gymnásium, i, n. / Lycéum, i, n.	*School (upper)*
Pegma, pégmatis, n.	*Shelves, bookcase*
Scirpículus, i	*Trash can*
Versus, us, m.	*Verse*

B. Commands / Exclamations Common in the Classroom

Sta / State!
Stand!

Sede / Sedéte!
Sit down!

Tace / Tacéte!
Be quiet!

Répete! Repétite! / Refer! Referte!
Repeat!

Scribe /Scríbite!
Write!

Alta voce lege / légite.
Read aloud.

Trade / Trádite mihi pensum.
Hand in the homework (to me).

Da mihi telephónum tuum! / Date mihi telephóna vestra!
Give me your phone! / Give me your phones!

Cape librum! / Cápite libros!
Take the book! / Take the books!

Depóne cálamum! / Depónite calamos!
Put down your pen! / Put down your pens!

Salúta / Salutáte condiscípulos.
Greet your classmates!

Róga / Rogáte amícos!
Ask your friends!

Veni / Veníte huc!
Come here!

I / Ite illúc!
Go over there!

Perge / Pérgite!
Continue!

Désine / Desínite!
Stop!

Bene!
Good!

Óptime!
Great!

Pulchre!
Nice! (lit. "Beautifully")

Certe!
Certainly!

C. Classroom Phrases

Suntne interrogánda?
Are there any questions?
Interrogándum est mihi.
I have a question.
Bonum interrogátum!
Good question!

Declína verbum "amo, amare"!
Conjugate the verb "amo, amare"!
Quid est "saepe"—verbum an advérbium?
What is "saepe"—a verb or adverb?

Ecce…!
Behold/Look…!
Quid téneo? Quid tenes?
What am I holding? What are you holding?

Nonne fábulam novam, magíster, tractáre debémus?
Shouldn't we go over a new story, teacher?
("Nonne" is used in questions whose expected answer is affirmative,
"num" in questions whose expected answer is negative.)

Mox revértar.
I'll be back (return) soon.
Quot discípuli adsunt / absunt?
How many students are present / are absent?

Nisi fallor, mox áderit Iúlia.
Unless I'm mistaken (or, I think) Julie will be here soon.

D. Time

i. Relative time

Ántea	Nunc	Póstea
Before, earlier	*Now*	*Later*

Matúre	Tempori / Ad tempus	In mora
Early	*On time*	*Late, tardily*

Paulo diútius
A little bit longer

Mox
Soon

Totus, a, um
Whole, entire

Proximus, a, um
Next (*but can also mean* previous)

Praeteritus, a, um
Previous, last

Unusquísque, unaquaéque, unumquódque
Each, every (*can also be expressed with* singuli, singulae, singula, *see example below*)

* Reminder: The ablative case is often used to indicate time. *
Véneris *die* omnes gaudémus.
On Friday we all rejoice.

Hora tertia discípuli domum redeunt.
At three o'clock students return home.

Tota nocte vigilávi!
I stayed up all night!

Proximo mense iter faciemus.
Next month we will go on a trip.

Unaquáque hebdómade probatiónem subímus! Eheu!
Síngulis hebdomádibus probatiónem subímus! Eheu!
We take a test every week! Alas!

ii. Days of the Week

Dies, diéi, m.
Day

Hébdomas, hebdómadis, f. / Septimána, ae, f.
Week

Solis dies / Domínicus dies	Lunae dies	Martis dies
Sunday	**Monday**	*Tuesday*

Mercúrii dies	Iovis dies	Véneris dies	Satúrni dies
Wednesday	*Thursday*	*Friday*	*Saturday*

Núdius tértius	Heri	Hódie	Cras	Postrídie
the day before yesterday	*yesterday*	*today*	*tomorrow*	*the day after tomorrow*

Quid hodie facis? / Quid hodie facit Marcus/Iulia?
What are you doing today? / What is Mark/Julie doing today?

iii. Months

mensis Ianuárius	*January*
mensis Februárius	*February*
mensis Mártius	*March*
mensis Aprílis	*April*
mensis Maius	*May*
mensis Iúnius	*June*
mensis Iúlius	*July*
mensis Augústus	*August*
mensis Septémber	*September*
mensis Octóber	*October*
mensis Novémber	*November*
mensis Decémber	*December*

Mensis, is, m.
Month

Annus, i, m.
Year

iv. *Minutes/Hours*

Hora, ae, f.
Hour

Moméntum temporis / Minúta, ae, f.
Minute

Hora prima cum quantránte
Quarter after 1:00, *i.e. 1:15*

Hora prima cum dimídia
Half past 1:00, *i.e. 1:30*

Hora prima cum dodránte
Quarter til 2:00, *i.e. 1:45*

Mane
In the morning

Merídies, meridiéi, m.
Noon

Tempus postmeridiánum
Afternoon

Vesper, vésperis, m.
Evening

Nox, noctis, f.
Night

v. Seasons

Ver, veris, n.
Spring

Aestas, aestátis, f.
Summer

Autúmnus, i, m.
Autumn

Hiems, híemis, f.
Winter

vi. Weather

Frígora sunt!
It's cold!

Calóres sunt!
It's hot!

Pluit!
It's raining!

Catervátim pluit!
It's raining a lot!

Urceátim pluit!
It's raining buckets!

Ningit!
It's snowing!

Ventus veheménter flat!
It's windy! (lit. "The wind is blowing strongly!")

Tonat!
It thunders!

Fulget!
There's lightning!

Caelum est serénum.
The sky is clear / calm.

Caelum est nubilósum.
The sky is cloudy.

Tempéstas, tempestátis, f.
Weather (or *storm*)

Pluvia, ae / Imber, imbris
Rain

Nix, nivis, f.
Snow

Tónitrus, us, m.
Thunder

Fulgor, fulgóris, m.
Lightning

E. Colors

Ruber, rubra, rubrum
Red

Caerúleus, a, um
Blue

Víridis, e
Green

Flavus, a, um
Yellow

Purpúreus, a, um
Purple

Niger, nigra, nigrum
Black

Albus, a, um
White

F. Food

Ientáculum, i
Breakfast

Prándium, i
Lunch

Cena, ae
Dinner

Cáffea, ae
Coffee

Esúrio, esuríre
To hunger

Sitio, sitíre
To thirst

Cómedo, comédere / Edo, esse
To eat

Bibo, bíbere
To drink

Esurísne? Sitísne?
Are you hungry? Are you thirsty?

Visne cáffea nobíscum frui?
Do you want to have (lit. "enjoy") coffee with us?

G. Grammatical Terms

Adiectívum, i, n. (nomen)
Adjective

Advérbium
Adverb

Casus, us, m.
Case

> Casus nominatívus
> *Nominative*

Casus genitívus
Genitive

Casus datívus
Dative

Casus accusatívus
Accusative

Casus ablatívus
Ablative

Casus vocatívus
Vocative

Declíno, declináre
To decline or conjugate

Coniugátio, coniugatiónis, f.
Conjugation

Coniúnctio, coniunctiónis, f.
Conjunction

Declinátio, declinatiónis, f.
Declension

Genus, géneris, n.
Gender

Femíneus, a, um
Feminine

Masculínus, a, um
Masculine

Neuter, neutra, neutrum
Neuter

Grammática, grammaticórum, n.
Grammar

Interiéctio, interiectiónis, f.
Interjection

Modus, i, m.
Mood

Modus imperatívus
Imperative

Modus indicatívus
Indicative

Modus infinitívus
Infinitive

Modus coniunctívus / subiunctívus
Subjunctive

Nomen substantívum
Noun

Númerus, i, m.
Number

Númerus singuláris
Singular

Númerus plurális
Plural

Singuláriter / Pluráliter tantum dícitur.
It is said only in the singular / plural.

Obiéctum, i, n.
Object

Períodus, i, f.
Sentence (*"sententia" usually refers to a proverb or maxim)*

Persóna, ae, f.
Person

> Prima persóna
> *First person*

> Secúnda persóna
> *Second person*

> Tértia persóna
> *Third person*

Praepósitio, praepositiónis, f.
Preposition

Radix, radícis, f.
Root

Sýllaba, ae, f. / Vox, vocis, f.
Syllable

> Antepaenúltima (sýllaba)
> *Antepenult*

Paenúltima (sýllaba)
Penult

Última (sýllaba)
Ultima

Sýllaba corrépta / Vox corrépta
Short syllable / Short vowel

Sýllaba prodúcta / Vox prodúcta
Long syllable

Tábula, ae, f.
Chart

Tempus, témporis, n.
Tense

Tempus praésens
Present tense

Tempus praetéritum imperféctum
Imperfect tense

Tempus praetéritum perféctum
Perfect tense

Tempus praetéritum plus quam perféctum
Pluperfect tense

Tempus futúrum
Future tense

Tempus futúrum perféctum
Future perfect tense

Verbum, i, n. / Vocábulum, i, n. / Vox, vocis, f.
Word

Verbum temporále
Verb

Vox actíva, vox passíva
Active voice, passive voice

Ending the Conversation: Goodbyes

Valéte, discípuli et discípulae!
Goodbye, students!

Vale, magíster (magístra)!
Goodbye, teacher!

In próximum!
See you soon!

In crástinum!
See you tomorrow!

Pausa hiemáli fruáris / fruámini!
Enjoy the winter break! (singular and plural)

Témpore vespertíno fruáris / fruámini!
Enjoy the evening!

Bonum iter tibi exópto!
I wish you a good trip!

Útinam mox convaléscas!
Get better soon!

Salúta Augústum meo nómine!
Say hello to Augustus for me!

Appendix 1

Using Latin Names

Choosing a Latin name

It's both fun and useful for students to have a Latin name in the classroom. Here are a few strategies for picking a Latin name:

1. **Choose a new name unrelated to your given name.** Many students love to take on a new identity as Livia, Augustus, or Caesar.
2. **Choose a name related to your first name.**
    a. **Based on meaning:** A student named Summer might be called Aestas.
    b. **Use the Latin cognate, if available:** "Julie" comes from the Roman name *Iulia*, "Mark" from *Marcus*.
3. **Choose a name related to your last name.** For example, a student with the last name Smith could be called Faber (a blacksmith); Miller could be Molinarius (a miller); Appleman could be Pomarius (a fruit seller).
4. **Choose a similar-sounding name.** Taylor could be Thalia, Darren could be Darius.
5. **Latinize a non-Latin name.**
    a. **Add first and second declension endings:** for females, -a, and for males, -us. For example, "Isaac" is a Hebrew name and often indeclinable in Latin (for example, in Vulgate). However, the form *Isaacus* is also used. Isaac Newton was known as Isaacus Newtonus in Latin.
    b. **Use the third declension.** "Michael" is another Hebrew name, but it is often in the third declension in Latin: Michael, Michaelis.
6. **Use a favorite Latin word as a name.** A student might like the word *Lux* or even *Lana*.

7. **Use a word that describes the student's personality or physical appearance:** for example, *Garrulus* (loud-mouthed) or *Parvulus* (very small).

Appendix 2

Vocatives

Remember to address students in the vocative case, which is identical to the nominative case with the exception of the second declension masculine, where the vocative form will end in -e in place of -us, unless it ends in -ius, in which case it will end in -i. In other words, female names don't generally change in the vocative, whereas many male names do.

Examples:
María, veni huc!
Mary, come here!

Marce, tace!
Mark (Marcus), be quiet!

Dari, quómodo te habes?
Darrell (Darius), how are you doing?

Míchael, cur irásceris?
Michael, why are you angry?

Heus amice, quo ámbulas?
Hey friend, where are you headed? *(addressing a male)*

Salve, amica!
Hello, friend. *(addressing a female)*

Appendix 3

Tips for Asking Questions

- **Open-ended personal questions:** Many students love talking about themselves. Ask them how they are doing, where they're from, what they like and dislike, what they want to do today, and so on.
- **Focused questions:** Specific material can be reinforced with the appropriate questions. Examples:
  o **Vocabulary:** Show a picture illustrating a scene from (or similar to) a story the students are reading, or reenact the scene (using students, puppets, etc.) and ask students what they see.
  o **Grammar:** Practice person by telling a student to do something and then asking that student, then others, what he or she is doing.
    Magistra: "Marce, sta! Quid facis?"
    Marcus: "Sto."
    Magistra: "María, quid facit Marcus?"
    Maria: "Marcus stat."
    The same practice can be used when teaching infinitives (e.g. "Quid vis facere?"), prepositions (e.g. "Quo ambulat?") etc. Many more examples of this can be found in the teacher's manuals by Peckett & Munday. (See the Bibliography.)
  o **Storytelling & "wh" questions:** When telling or reading a story, frequently stop and ask the *who, what, when, where, why, how* questions.
- **Metalanguage:** For example, ask students to identify a part of speech: "Estne *audítor* verbum temporále, an nomen substantívum?" Ask them to identify noun case: "Quo casu est hoc nomen substantívum?" And so forth.
- **Take turns:** Have students ask the instructor and each other questions.

- **Plan ahead:** Come to class with a variety of questions written down for a particular lesson.

Appendix 4

Interrogatives

Quis? quid?
Who?

	Masc. & Fem.	*Neut.*
Nom. Sg.	quis? *who?*	quid? *what?*
Gen. Sg.	cuius? *whose?*	
Dat. Sg.	cui? *to/for whom? / what?*	
Acc. Sg.	quem? *whom?*	quid? *what?*
Abl. Sg.	quo? *from/with/in/by whom? / what?*	

	Masc.	*Fem.*	*Neut.*
Nom. Pl.	qui? *who?*	quae? *who? / what?*	
Gen. Pl.	quorum? *of whom?*	quarum? *of whom?*	quorum? *of what?*
Dat. Pl.	quibus? *to whom? / what?*		
Acc. Pl.	quos? *whom?*	quas? *whom?*	quae? *what?*
Abl. Pl.	quibus? *from/with/in/by whom? / what?*		

Quis? quae? quod?
Which? *(declined the same as above except for these nominative singular forms)*

Ecquis? ecquae? ecquod?
... anyone / anything ... ?
Ecquis cálamum méum vidit?
Has anyone seen my pen?

Qualis? quale?
What is ___ like?
Qualis est haec puella? Laeta est haec puella.
What is this girl like? This girl is happy.

Quantus, quanta, quantum?
How great / large?

Quam ___? *(with an adjective or adverb)*
How ___?
Quam díligens est Marcus?
How hardworking is Marcus?
Quam saepe aegrótas?
How often do you get sick?

Cur?
Why?

Quomodo?
How?

Quot?
How many?

Quóties?
How many times?

Ubi?
Where?

Unde?
From where? Whence?

Quo?
To where? Whither?

Quando?
When?

Quota hora?
At what time?

Bibliography:

Print Resources

Albert, Sigrides. *Imaginum Vocabularium Latinum.* 2nd ed.
Saraviponti, Saarbräcken: Pegaus, 2009.

Collins, John F. *A Primer of Ecclesiastical Latin.* Washington, D.C.:
Catholic University of America Press, 1988.

HarperCollins Latin Concise Dictionary & Grammar. Glasgow,
HarperCollins, 2005.

Henle, R. J. *Latin Grammar for High Schools.* Chicago: Loyola
University Press, 1945.

Maier, Robert and Kerstin Klingelhöffer. *Visuelles Wörterbuch:
Latein - Deutsch: über 6000 Wörter und Redewendungen.*
München: Dorling Kindersley, 2010.

Peckett, C. W. E. and A. R. Munday. *A Basic Latin Grammar.*
London: Rivingtons, 1966.

_____. *Principia: A Beginner's Latin Course, Part One.*
Shrewsbury: Wilding and Son, 1969.

_____. Pseudolus noster: *A Beginner's Latin Course, Part Two.*
Shrewsbury: Wilding and Son, 1972.

Traupman, John C. *Conversational Latin for Oral Proficiency:
Phrase Book and Dictionnary.* 3rd ed. Wauconda, Ill.:
Bolchazy-Carducci, 2008.

Wheelock, Fredric M. and Richard A. LaFleur. *Wheelock's Latin*.
       7th ed. New York: CollinsReference, 2009.

Online Resources:

Lexicon Morganium: JosephSusanka.com/latin

Logeion: logeion.uchicago.edu/index.html